Fifty Shots at Game

Erotica For The Overly Ind

WARNING: This book contains graphic

Please don't look if you are easily offended

Follow the continuing humour @50shotsatgame

Copyright © 2015 C.L Grey All rights reserved

The right of C.L Grey to be identified as the author of this work has been asserted by them in accordance with the Copyright, Designs and Patents Act 1988

All rights reserved. Apart from any permitted use under UK Copyright Law. No part of this publication may be reproduced or transmitted in any form or by any means, electrical or mechanical, including photocopying, recording or any storage or retrieval system, without permission in writing from the publisher or under licence from the Copyright Licencing Agency Limited. Further details of such licences (for reprographic reproduction) may be obtained from the Copyright Licencing Agency Ltd, Saffron House, 6-10 Kirby Street, London EC1N 8TS

First Published in 2015 by Callum Grey

ISBN-13: 978-1519278869
ISBN-10: 1519278861

Disclaimer: FIFTY SHOTS AT GAME: by C.L Grey, is not prepared, authorised, licensed, approved or endorsed by any person or entity involved in the making of the E. L. James' FIFTY SHADES OF GREY series of books, motion pictures or associated productions.

All characters and events in this publication, other than those clearly in the public domain, are fictitious and any resemblance to real persons, living or dead is purely coincidental.

Available from Amazon.com, CreateSpace.com, and other retail outlets.

Contents

Acknowledgements 4
Chance Encounter 5
Home 7
Hide and Seek 9
Ménage-et-Trois 11
Strip Please 13
An Invitation for a Days Driven Pheasant 15
Sandford 17
Drive 1 – Willies Clump 19
Pepper 20
Drive 2 – Jane's Backdoor 21
Elevenses 22
Drive 3 – Cherry Pie 24
Drive 4 – Hidden Garden 26
Game Card 28
Evening Flight 29
Easing It In 31

Acknowledgements

I owe a huge debt of thanks to many people for a variety of reasons:

To all those who have welcomed me in the shooting community over the numerous years, at many shoot days, charity and social events. Your passion for field sports is unwavering and inspiring. Long may it continue and I hope to spend even more days on peg, in your company.

My children, crazy, loving and forever giving me reason to continue to try and replenish the bank balance. I am immensely proud of you all.

To my long suffering wife, who not only puts up with my obsession with game shooting, hours of stalking and absence from home to roll around in fields, but also motivated and supported me to continue with my writing. Thank you for being my best friend, stunningly gorgeous and pretty good at loading to. You can stay another season.

Chance Encounter

I stood in the centre of the room. Transfixed with all the surrounding paraphernalia and toys at my disposal. A surge of excitement was coursing through my veins faster than cocaine travels up a celebrity's £50 note.

Through the floor to ceiling windows, I could see the reflection of the bright, July summer sun, glistening off the roof of my Range Rover. Blurred vapours of heat rose from its bonnet, slightly distorting the image of open farmland behind it.

I hate the summer. I detest the frivolity and laziness of it.

Bring on the autumn. Hurry along and taint the leaves golden brown and decline the temperature. Wash me with cold, stinging, English rain and biting frosts that enliven the nerve endings like a back handed slap from the house prefect.

The gun room at Frankie Lottrell's is quite superb, adorned with lashings of walnut, sumptuous leather and polished metals. It could be a Madame's dungeon.

Across the back wall I surveyed several items of temptation. All in perfect alignment and pristine. Shotguns, in 50 shades of grey, black and brown, handcrafted and engraved by master craftsmen.

But then, I froze. Totally absorbed in the image captured by my eyes. She was an image of total elegance and I was transfixed instantly. Her subtle elegance drew me in like a training collar on a spaniel. I had to have her. Right then, right now and forever.

Christ, I hope I have remembered my shotgun certificate.

Home

We pulled up the driveway after a winding stint along the beautiful Cotswolds lanes. Montgomery was waiting on the steps to the house and I knew I couldn't pull straight into the garage. He's such a lovely chap and has been with us since as long as I can remember. He always parks the car when I return and fetches it to the door in the mornings. But he's been warned to keep me from my vices and I cannot entertain his dull lectures today.

"I'll have to sneak you in" I whispered to her, out of the corner of my mouth.

I waved at Montgomery and pointed to the garage as I lowered the window. Trying to think quickly.

"Afternoon Monty"

"Good afternoon Sir" he replied. Standing bolt upright, his suit and shoes pristine.

"Monty, I have to erm... I have to check the screenwash on the car, no need to park her up, I'll take her over to the garage" He looked rather bemused.

"Sir, I will.." he started

"Monty, its fine" I interrupted swiftly. "I can manage. Anyhow, some tea is in order I feel"

"Very well Sir" he replied turning instantly on his heel with a snap. That's Monty all over. Efficient, reliable and extremely amiable. A perfect butler who is also a dear friend.

"Monty." I called after him.

"Sir" he turned so fast, I thought his legs would shatter.

"Your fly is undone old chap" I exclaimed.

Instantly his face reddened but otherwise he remained perfectly still, like the statues on the lawn.

"My apologies Sir. I will rectify the situation immediately" he replied, unwaveringly. Then he turned and was off again.

Ménage-et-Trois

Just one week to the first driven pheasant day of the season and Monty had been full of surprises. The tailor had arrived in good time for the final fitting of my tweed suit. I felt a fine pattern was in order this season, reflective of my father's design, but the samples looked and felt nothing like what I wanted to clothe myself in. Monty, somehow had managed to track down an early example of my father's design. He produced it, unannounced and with his understated generosity at the tailors shop. Good old fellow. I almost felt bad for telling him earlier that morning that I had cancelled his holiday. He was needed to assist Billy the gardener with moving the compost pile, further away from the summer house. I don't think he had anything planned. But that smell was causing an awful nuisance whilst entertaining.

I had taken Sophia out at every opportunity. I was really enjoying our time together and she seemed to find it easy to pleasure me. When I had her in my arms, it just felt so natural, so perfect. We had spent a great deal of time together at the clay shooting ground. But this day turned out to be somewhat special.

On the forth stand, I ran into Nicole. A pert, young, firecracker of a girl who's over exuberance in vocalisation of nigh on every aspect of her life, was equal only to her ability to shoot. For a twenty something, she could put most guns to shame on any sporting round of clays. But as her father owned the shooting ground, she had more or less been raised with a 12 gauge in one hand and a Sloe Gin in the other.

"Hello Callum" she giggled, embracing me with a wonderfully broad smile and sparkling eyes. "Long time no see".

"Nicole, lovely to see you again" I started, avoiding asking how life was. I only had an hour to spare. Not Four

"Yes, likewise" she replied, her eyes dropping to my waist.

"Oh. Callum!" she paused eyeing everything but my pupils. "New gun?"

"Yes, yes, stunning isn't she?" pride swept over me as I introduced Sophia who was on my arm.

"Yeah, those are some gorgeous lines. May I?" she placed her broken shotgun in the stand and extended a hand to Sophia.

I instantly became wary. Nicole can be a little rough.

"Uh, sure of course" I stammered, nervously letting Sophia be led away by Nicole.

Nicole was far tenderer with her touch than I expected. She gazed at Sophia in admiration. Biting her lip as she turned her over, exploring every inch of her form. Touching, stroking, her curves. Expertly, Nicole firmly held Sophia, opening her up, exposing her. I could see in her other hand that she was rolling her fingers around a short plastic shaft and brass tipped love slug. My pulse quickened.

I could only watch in awe and the two of them rocked back and forth. Sophia responding to Nicole's every wanton touch. Nicole gaining pace and confidence as Sophia pushed closer with every thrust. Each shockwave causing Nicole's breasts to heave up and down under her polo shirt. Crikey.

I've always advocated shooting vests for the ladies.

Strip Please

Everything was prepared. Monty had the night off and I was sure we wouldn't be disturbed.

The fine mahogany table was strewn with soft cloth. The reading lamp cast a soft orange glow across the study and faint wisps of some unknown folk artist drifted invisibly, bounced with gentle springs off every surface, from the Bose system to my ear drum. Scents of oil vapours encased the room and tingled as I breathed them in deeply, closing my eyes and consuming the atmosphere.

"It's just us" I thought to myself. "You're a dirty girl and you need cleansing"

I took Sophia, uncovered and exposed to the orange glow from the lights and laid her gently over the table. There was still a sparkle from her but I knew that by the end of this evening, she would be radiating light.

Lifting her slightly, I cupped my hand underneath, slightly fumbling for the clasp. But seeking it out with my fingers I released it and her fore came away in my warm, soft hands. Gently now, I tiptoed my fingers to her top lever and pressed firmly. Instantly, she made herself open for me.

I knew what needed to be done. Tentatively at first, I took my rod and squeezed it into her, making sure it penetrated to its full length. I withdrew, leaving the tip just in and pressed back again, firmer, faster.

For a solid 5 minutes both her barrels got a good thrusting with my rod. Then I finished her off by rubbing lubricant and oil, in all her sticky places.

I had oil and deposits all over my hands and sweat on my brow, I felt spent.

Bloody hell, the state of the cloth! Stains and oily marks everywhere. Monty will be on to us.

An Invitation for a Days Driven Pheasant

His Lordship Cornelius Barble-Fuq, the 17th Earl of Sandford, cordially invites you to attend a days shooting at the Sandford Estate.

Dear *Callum*,

Our first driven day of the pheasant season is upon us. Nothing beats England in autumn, its trees like burning torches, set ablaze with leaves of orange and crimson against the typical dull grey skies.

My estate is set amongst 9,000 acres of beautiful rolling hills and fields set in the deepest 'Cotswoldy' countryside and boasts some of the country's greatest pheasant and partridge drives.

I do hope you would be able to accept and attend.

Fellow guns in the line will include;

Tarquin Smythe-Crackelhoar, a fine gent whose great, great grandfather had made his fortune importing tea.

Hugo Lympwryster, property investor and entrepreneur.

Charlie Coq-Frais, the renowned Michelin starred restauranteur and wine aficionado.

Sebastian Leong-Johnson, following in his family's heritage of arable farming over thousands of acres.

Tobias Winstanley, old Etonian, all-round good egg and race horse breeder.

Hans Flickenballz, a dear friend from the Black Forest in Germany.

Dave, for every team needs a Dave.

This 500 bird day will be one to remember. You may, of course, bring your own loaders and drivers, alternatively the Estate has access to a number of professionals should you require them. Your invitation is extended to the evening as guest of the great house.

Please arrive promptly at 09:00 at the Estate helipad or shoot office.

Warmest regards *Cornelius*

Sandford

We touched down in the field just behind the shoot lodge. The helicopter ride was a brief 30 minute journey but enabled me to leave Monty at the Great House. He was rather unwell, poor old chap, so a day off was the order of the day. It also allowed for me to sneak Sophia into the helicopter for our first driven game expedition.

After exchanging pleasantries with my fellow guns and eating the obligatory bacon rolls for breakfast it was time for the briefing. Eddy, our Head Keeper laid out the rules of engagement for the day.

"Gentlemen, pheasant and partridge are the main order for today, no pigeon or ground game are allowed. You may see a few Woodcock. Naturally, if the shot is clean and safe you may also shoot at those. A whistle will be used to commence a drive, please only go live on peg and you will also hear a hunting horn at the end of the drive. No shooting after this!" he stated sternly. "This is a 400 bird day, we'll do our best to get them over you in this wind. Have a fantastic but safe day."

Eddy struck me as a sturdy fellow, no doubt his solid 6ft 7inch frame had been shaped and moulded by many of his 20 plus years, building holding pens, working his team of dogs and walking hundreds of miles over the shoot.

"Good morning Mr Grey" a familiar melodic female tone trickled over my shoulder and into my ear.

"Ah, Nicole. Good morning to you to. What do I owe this pleasure?" I said, turning to see her radiance. Fitted out in matching tweed jacket and breeks over crimson shooting socks, her curvaceous figure was accentuated in all the right places.

"I'm loading for you today" she giggled, biting her lip and flashing her bright eyes at me from under the rim of her hat.

Her dark chocolate, tousled hair draping downward from her fedora, curling and entwining like the most glorious engraved scrollwork on a side plate. Instantly, I thought of Sophia and what was going to happen between the three of us.

"Superb. But I must tell you, I have very specific needs. When I want you to…. I want you to do it hard and fast. Don't fumble, or the moment is lost" I demanded.

"Oh, Callum" she gasped, reeling. "What would you do with me if I did fumble?"

I glared deep into her ice blue firestorm pupils.

"Well, you certainly won't be getting a tip."

Drive 1 – Willies Clump

Arriving on peg, Nicole and I immediately started to prepare for the first drive of the day. Deep in a bowl with woodland to our backs and dog leg of various trees lining the edge of the bowl, with a crop of maize stood behind, I anticipated Nicole would need fast hands and quick wrist action to satisfy my demand.

"Try to keep your hands warm" I suggested to her. "The cold will slow us both down and delay my shot".

"I can handle it Mr Grey" she quipped, half certain. I sensed her frustration with me.

"Apologies Nicole. I'm sure you can. The thing is, my timing has been a little off lately and emptying my barrels rather prematurely. It has made me rather frustrated." It took a lot to admit that to her.

"Well," she replied with a warmth that exuded empathy and condolence. "No gentleman wants to shoot his load to soon, it can be embarrassing for everyone involved. I have seen it happen a few times in the field"

For the next twenty minutes, Sophia, Nicole and I had some frantic action together. Nicole purposely slowing me down at times, driving the rhythm like a conductor of an orchestra. It was a symphony that ebbed and flowed. At the climax there was the traditional blowing of the horn and I was exhausted.

Pepper

We started to head back toward the Gun's trailer. Nicole could see I was drained.

"Shall I hold your cock for you" Nicole whispered.

"Certainly" I replied, handing it over, "Can you take this hen as well? I've a habit of falling of stiles"

We gathered for a quick nip and to recount the stories of the first drive. Back slapping and joviality ensued, then it was back into the trailer and then brisk transportation to the next drive.

Sat in the trailer, Pepper a friend of Tobias, started to press herself up against me. He could see it happening but was too engrossed in his conversation. She kept on nudging closer, and I knew it would be just a matter of time before I would have to roll her over and run my hands all over her, to satisfy her demands for affection.

I looked into her big brown eyes and I think she knew it to... she is a gorgeous Labrador.

Drive 2 – Jane's Backdoor

According to Cornelius, Jane's Backdoor had seen a lot of action over the years. Many men had visited the estate to stand and bang away for countless hours in its expansive setting. They always left satisfied after emptying their bags. Some of the hardest cocks had been seen in Jane's Backdoor and quite honestly, I was right up for it myself. Even after my earlier session with Nicole and Sophia had left me so weary.

Nicole took Sophia from me and we made our way to peg 6. We'd been on the outer edge of Jane's Backdoor, but I'm sure we'd still get stuck in.

Not long after the whistle sounded commencement of the drive, pheasants and partridge were filling the air and soaring over the centre of the line. Nicole was like a child in a sweet shop

"Wood..cock!" she shouted excitedly. I was puzzled as to how she knew. I was facing away the other way. Perhaps the cold hadn't affected me this morning.

I swung Sophia around and gave her a squeeze. She let out her usual cackle and I dropped the aerial acrobat at around 45 yards.

I'd never forget my first visit to Jane's Backdoor and how satisfying it felt firing my load in there.

Elevenses

The grey skies had begun to weep a little drizzle on the day's proceedings. Coupled with the biting wind, elevenses became a welcome break. The gun's trailer had taken us past beautiful fields and woodland before it pulled up to the shoot lodge. This is what a day in the field should be like.

Stepping down from the trailer, I turned up my collar against the wind and strode onward towards the inner warmth of the lodge. The roaring log burner in the room casting invisible rays of heat, invitingly pulling me in.

The game cart was over flowing and one of the shoot helpers was busying himself tying and counting brace. I stopped for a moment. Something didn't feel right, I knelt down. Quickly, I groped at their breasts, warm and full. Somewhere beneath the pile of hen birds, I'd dropped my dog whistle.

"Mr Grey, there's something quite attractive about seeing you on your knees" Nicole smartly commented. Playfully smiling with cheeks reddened by the cold.

"There would be something quite attractive about seeing you on yours Ms Peele" I could not believe I had let that creep out unwittingly.

Nicole paused, only momentarily, her face even more flushed in a hearty glow.

"Well Mr Grey...... I never thought you licked this side of the stamp?" she asked with a wry smile.

"Ms Peele, just because I do not surround myself with young ladies, do not be mistaken. There is only one team I bat for. I just don't do the girlfriend thing."

Drive 3 – Cherry Pie

Having quaffed several glasses of Sloe Gin and Champagne it was time to steady myself on the peg. Nicole had been somewhat quiet on the way to the peg. Perhaps, I had overstepped the mark.

Cherry Pie was reportedly a superb partridge drive. Beside me on their peg were Hans and Sebastian, both exuberant and full of excitement from the morning's action. Nicole, skulked in beside me and placed Sophia in my palm.

"Nicole, I'm.."

"No don't Callum" she interrupted. "I'm sorry I didn't mean to cause offense by questioning your sexual persuasion." She began to well up.

"Nicole, honestly, it's no issue. I felt I had offended you by making a flirtatious remark." The fear of upsetting her had already begun to crawl through my veins.

"Actually Callum. I rather liked it" she said softly, almost drowned out by the whistle. Or at least that's what I thought she said.

"Pardon, Nicole say that again?" I asked

"I rather….." she started BOOM Sophia's first barrel interrupted her as I knocked down a cock bird who was quartering to my left.

"Sorry Nicole, please go on" I requested pointing Sophia forward and at in incoming partridge.

"I said I r…" BOOM, bloody hell that partridge folded at about 35 yards out.

"What?" I said as Nicole slid in beside me, easing two more fun slugs into Sophia.

"I said, I RATHER LIKED IT" she shouted, attempting to get her message to me over the now non existent gun fire.

"OK Nicole." I scolded her "There's no need to bloody shout" I slighted through gritted teeth.

Settling my cheek back on to Sophia, I was strangely excited by Nicole's revelation.

Drive 4 – Hidden Garden

Nestled in one far corner of the Sandford Estate we were trailered into position. With the tally of shots and birds mounting, this next drive proved to be the most spectacular of the day.

In the ruins of a previous second mansion house on the estate, we were surrounded by short stone walls and the remnants of the old buildings landscaped grounds. With pines tress, laurels and overgrown brambles providing plenty of cover in the rolling hill overlooking the gun line, the tight spaces would call for snap shooting galore.

By now, my shoulder was feeling the pressure from Sophia's regular and overly frequent embrace from today. But banging away with her was something I could not resist. This drive, I knew would bring us closer to total unci.

"These are very attractive grounds" I muttered to Nicole who was looking somewhat forlorn since the last drive.

"Yes, they are" she said, fiddling with her muff.

"That's a lovely looking muff!" I motioned toward her waist, where she had folder her arms inside the fur lined garment. "It's such a shame this garden has gone to waste though, isn't it?" Nicole, was beginning to brighten up again, her smile creeping back into the corners of her ever so full and sweet lips.

"Yes. Apparently, many years ago, the old lady who lived here, had a team of men tending to her garden. As the years went by they left, each having exhausted themselves keeping it trim and fit. As such it became dilapidated and went to complete ruin in her later years." she stated, gazing around with an air of nostalgia. "It's why I keep my secret garden simple and clean. No bush to tend to. I'm even considering removing the thin strip of lawn."

"Well, that's understandable" I replied, taking a sharp intake of the cold, afternoon air. "I've seen some lovely garden's, both with and without a wicket to play on"

124 Pheasant and 15 Partridge fell to the gun line on that drive.

Game Card

Guns	Bag
Cornelius Barble –Fug	Pheasant 337
Tarquin Smythe-Crackelhoar	Partridge 75
Callum Grey	
Hans Flickenballz	Woodcock 5
Hugo Lympwryster	Total 417
Charlie Coq-Frais	**Drives**
Tobias Winstanley	Willies Clump
Sebastian Leong-Johnson	Jane's Backdoor
Dave	Cherry Pie
	Hidden Garden

Date............October 31ˢᵗ 2015..........................

Evening Flight

Dinner had been served, the food and banter was simply irresistible. As a team of unfamiliar guns, generous bonds had been made throughout the day which inevitably lead to the opportunistic ceasing of moments to rib one another. Around the dinner table these came to the fore. Cornelius was on top form, as he recounted the day's highest birds and some of the more memorable moments witnessed from the line. The warmed port was beginning to flow and soon it was time to bid my farewells. Tipping the head keeper Eddy and making my way to the edge of the grounds I noticed Nicole lingering close to the gun trailer. She had Sophia draped over her shoulder, protected from the cold.

"I've taken good care of her for you" Nicole smiled sweetly. "After all, that was a hefty day of swinging and banging."

"Absolutely and thank you" I replied, slightly unbalanced by the various alcoholic libations I had consumed.

"I've cleaned and oiled her for you. She will be ready for your next wanton session." My mind began to visualise Nicole's slender hands and delicate touch smoothing and encasing Sophia's full lengthy profile. I felt an instant stirring in my trousers.

"Apologies Nicole, that's my phone vibrating" I excused myself and answered the call from the pilot of the helicopter stating he was ready for my return journey. "Nicole, would you like to travel back with me?" I asked without thinking.

"Oh, I don't know Mr Grey" she paused, biting her lip. "I've never been in a helicopter before" she looked for the first time like a nervous, yet excited child at the foot of the world's largest rollercoaster. I took her hand in mine. Heat radiated from her finger tips and sent a shockwave through my arm.

"Shit" she yelped, pulling herself off the electric fence.

"Here, are you okay" I asked urgently, fearing she may be injured or harmed.

"Oh I've don't it a million times at the stables, still makes me curse though, apologies."

"No need to apologise. Well? Would you like to come back with me? We can drop you in the field opposite the clay ground." I felt suddenly eager to retain her closeness and enjoy more time in her company.

"Erm…. Yes. Yes please, that would be fantastic but I…" she hesitated

"You're a little nervous aren't you" I could sense the adrenaline flowing through her body.

"Yes a little" she confessed, her pulse rate increasing.

"Would you care to join me in a drink ahead of the flight then? A little Dutch courage, so to speak?" I was starting to feel the cold and felt a nip would probably do us both the world of good. Reaching to my jacket pocket I retrieved my hip flask full with Kings Ginger.

"Thank you that would be great" she replied, placing her red full lips to the rim and taking a long sip. I watched her as my warming liquid slid down her throat and caused its inevitable spicy glow to raise and surge through her core. Her face flushed and it spread across her ivory neck turning it to subtle shades of pink and crimson. "Oh, my" she reeled slightly, staring at my vessel.

"First time?" I pondered.

"Yes, that was quite unexpected" she giggled.

That signalled time to board the helicopter.

Easing It In

Circling round the clay shooting grounds, Roger the pilot, mentioned a growing gusty cross wind but reassured us of his confidence. I had flown with him many times before and knew his skill as a pilot was unquestionable.

"Roger, roger" I replied on the internal radio set. Nicole giggled, still peering out of the window, entranced by her first flight.

A little static fill our earphones as Roger opened up his mic.

"Mr Grey, I'm going to set down just a little further in the field, I'll do my best to ease it in and touch down gently" his slightly distorted, but cool as a cucumber voice resonated inside the plastic cans over my head. Nicole was off giggling again. But she had finished off the Kings Ginger. I gazed at her with growing affection and admiration.

Once down and rotors almost stationary Roger assisted us from the cockpit and I began to escort Nicole across the field.

"What tickled you so much?" I queried.

"Roger roger wants to ease it in" she chuckled, heady from the flight and ginger liquor that had reduced her inhibitions.

"Quite. But if you want to roger, Roger, I'm afraid you'll have to have to make some significant changes" I replied with a knowing wink.

"Sorry Callum. I don't follow" she paused.

"Roger, likes to be roger'd" I said. Staring back at her elegant face.

"Oooh. I see. Roger does bat for the other team" she replied. "Shame, the rumour of all the good looking guys being gay, does appear to be true"

"I take it that you feel I am unattractive then?" I teased. As I did, Nicole suddenly lost her footing on the wet field and I grasped her close to my chest, preventing her falling. It felt unusual to hold her so close, but also, so right. She stared up at me as she raised her head from my chest. I swept a few wisps of hair from her face.

"Oh Callum. If only you would open your eyes and see what is around you" she murmured as she looked up at me. I felt like she was looking right at my very soul.

"Am I stood in a cow pat."

50 Shot Loads

C L Grey

`The much anticipated follow up to 50 Shots At Game, quirky, greater depth and more laughs' *No-one just yet as I haven't paid them*

It is only ten days since Callum Grey took Nicole on a whirlwind ride across the English countryside and sparked a fire that burned in both their bodies. Now, he is in turmoil; bewitched and unable to recognise the changes the young woman is making to his life and his personal judgement – Grey has been hurt before and doesn't know how to react to her advances.

Grey works best when his passions are up, when he focuses on a target and blasts with his enormous barrels. Here though, his love for all things country and sporting will drive him to discover new pleasures and experiment in unchartered waters. Is he out of his depth................

`Packed with tension, humour, field sports references and an attention to the daily grind of a wealthy game shot who is blessed with man servants, acres of land and superfluous riches. It also boasts shocking and satisfying multiple climaxes for the ladies' *Dave*

ISBN-13: 978-1519596253

ISBN-10: 1519596251

Printed in Great Britain
by Amazon.co.uk, Ltd.,
Marston Gate.